Being U 4 Real!

Carmen Thomas

ISBN: 0615767532
ISBN-13: 978-0615767536

Published & Distributed By:
Carmen Thomas, Legacy, ULTD

Cover Design & Formatting:
NyShell Imari Unlimited
www.nyshellimari.com

PRAISES FOR "BEING U 4REAL!"

I have had the privilege of knowing Carmen for about 40 years and we have been on some of the same up and down roads of finding ourselves. One thing we have always had in common and that is we were taught to care about people and as we really began to develop our relationship with God we saw how he kept us in the midst of our low times in life. Reader, trust Carmen as she takes you on a journey of life and loving yourself no matter what season of life you are in. If you have felt like no one has ever encouraged you allow Carmen to be that encouragement to help you Be U and Do U 4real.
-**Darshann Stevenson**, Lansing, MI

The underlying theme that is consistent in Carmen's life is that she is passionate about helping others achieve their dreams. In *Being U 4 Real*, she is transparent about her life in order to inspire others to truly be themselves. Carmen takes readers on a journey where she shares wisdom and life lessons while challenging them to learn, discover, and grow. This book is a must read for those who desire to live intentionally.
-**Elaine Harris**, Southfield, MI

Everything I read in Carmen's book tackles treating various types of individuals with low self-esteem. The book's analogy really helps the reader overcome low self-esteem and live a complimentary life. In reading this book you will understand being authentic is the best choice of life. I strongly endorse this book and challenge readers to seize a full and authentic life that encompass the removal of doubt and self-pity.
-**Apostle Carolyn Edwards**, Chicago, IL

Carmen Thomas has a remarkable ability to impart insight and wisdom. She is gifted and perfectly suited to help women become their best and most authentic selves. In this book she shares her experiences transparently with the hope of liberating others from the emotional prison of low self-esteem and bad choices.

Carmen has done the hard work of detaching herself from people and situations that were counterproductive to her growth, and redirected her multiple intelligences towards achieving her life purpose. The level of success she now walks in is astonishing and very inspirational.
With a clearly defined mission and her destiny in view, she is truly unstoppable!
-Evangelist Rahshaan Watson, Lansing, MI

The opening pages of Carmen's book took my breath away. I am inspired by her point of view on self-esteem and character building. It is evident that she exhibited many life experiences in the topics she writes about. The family dynamics used were unique mechanisms to offer creative ideas and advice to the common reader. I admire her soft yet gentle words chosen to balance between life circumstances and reality. I'm elated to endorse this book!
-Kim Milton, Lansing, MI

By learning how to walk in "My Authenticity 4Real while Being & Doing U" is the most important thing a person can do to live a lifestyle that is not mediocre but rich and fulfilling. Carmen Thomas has a deep understanding of living an authentic lifestyle, which she shares to help people begin to live out their lives by "Being U 4Real" with her new book. The reader will begin to put into practice the steps listed in the book to be their authentic self.

Carmen Thomas does not write simply from knowledge but her own personal experience and passionate desires to know her authentic self. Her challenges and successes in life have allowed her to discover the belief and commitment that has helped her to become an outstanding Christian, a wonderful wife and mother, a successful businesswoman, contributor in the community and a great loving friend.

Her unique and interesting style of writing keeps the reader involved in the book until it has been fully assimilated. This is one of those books that will be life changing for everyone that reads and follow the prescribed directions. Thanks, Carmen Thomas, for finishing this book. Your reward will be great, as multitudes of people around the world change their lives by reading and implementing your book and becoming their Authentic Self 4Real.
-**Tonyan L Poole-Geans**, Winter Springs, FL

This book brings clarity and balance to your life in terms of developing a healthy self-esteem. The author illustrates what a healthy self-esteem entails by clearly defining that it is neither being heady minded—whereas becoming overly confident in ones abilities nor is it being insecure due to inexperience because of lack of knowledge or confidence in oneself. Yet instead, it brings equilibrium within each individual's mindset by defining who you are and providing insight on how you can successfully function in this world victoriously through recognizing your power within by thinking on thoughts that produce positive results.

The author of this book is not foreign to the woes of low self-esteem issues because she writes from experience and has successfully conquered its mind binding control. However, the book reflects that we fail because of failure to believe that we can do all things through Christ who strengthens us. Although this book emphasizes Christian principles, it can be applied to all aspects of your life. It will help the reader to capably function with a reassuring confidence of who God has created him/her to be on this earth as an earth shaker and history maker. Additionally, the tools provided in this book are designed to help you change your thought life concerning who you are. These tools can be used over and over again in every area of your life.

After reading this book and applying the principles provided, you will undoubtedly find that it is a proven fact that when you change your thought life from a negative to a positive way of thinking; you will experience a victorious and a quality of life. Furthermore, the revelation knowledge that the author expresses in this book will set you free from the demeaning and destructive mindsets that have perverted your way of thinking and have prevented you from operating and exhibiting a healthy self-esteem. I believe the author will be amazed and grateful to God at the number of people that will experience healing and deliverance at great levels from the spirit of doubt and unbelief in oneself after reading this book.

Ultimately, this book will transform and empower the reader to see themself as God sees them, as a favorable and invaluable contributor to their community because God sees greatness in you. This book will also prompt the reader to inspire others to confidently love, respect, trust and believe in oneself in order to accomplish those great exploits that God has predestined them to achieve, by His power.

-Gloria Pearl Jones, Lansing, Michigan

In a world where one can easily lose their true sense of self by trying to "fit in" or end up being over shadowed by trying to "please others," Carmen Thomas has taken the subject of "Self Esteem" to another level through her step by step process of addressing the issue of being real with one's self, while discovering your true sense of worth and value. It is a heartfelt journey, which will cause you to open up and dig deeper to the treasure of being who you really are.
-Rev. Rebekah Lemley

Carmen is a Godly woman who loves truth. She is a motivator, visionary, innovator and courageous leader. She has held positions in organizations, businesses and ministries. She has taken the courage and tenacity to be transparent with her life and this book.

Carmen is encouraging and supporting women to take this opportunity to be free from any limitations to grow and become all that God has created them to be in their God given purpose.
-Laquetta Smith, Kalamazoo, MI

In all the years I've known Carmen she has always been transparent and authentic. She is a woman who is very confident in who she is in her marriage, as a mother, and in her career and business ventures. Carmen has a passion for helping people, especially women, develop their self-esteem. Her successful life speaks volumes about learning how to be the person you were created to be.
- Latissa Dozier

WHY THIS BOOK?

I want every woman to know who they are in Christ 4Real and walk out their God given purpose and destiny here on earth!

I am writing this book for every woman that:
- ❖ Ever felt rejected; know that you can be accepted.
- ❖ Ever felt depressed; know that you can have joy.
- ❖ Ever had low self-esteem; know who you are in Christ.
- ❖ Ever wondered what your purpose is; know that you have a purpose in Christ.

I am writing this book for our mothers, sisters, daughters, granddaughters, aunts, nieces, cousins and girlfriends.

I am happy to know that we all have the opportunity to be the best God called us to be. We do not have to settle for anything less! We don't have to compromise our authentic identity. We had a purpose before we were ever created and it is totally up to us to pursue our purpose.

Unstoppable Kingdom Builders!!!

CONTENTS

About Me:
My Authenticity 4Real

Being U 4REAL is a journey. It's a journey of learning from your past, embracing your present and planning your future. I would like to first start off with some background information about me.

My mother raised four children as a single mother, my dad died when I was about twelve years old and I was the oldest child. I remember growing up and living in both projects on each side of the city we lived in. Despite her circumstances, my mother did not allow the setback of raising four children hinder her from pursuing her dreams. Instead of quitting, giving up or throwing in the towel she chose to press in and pursue better things for herself and her family.

The last major move I had during my childhood was from the projects into a home my mother had built - she currently resides in that home today. My mother eventually went back to school and earned a Bachelor's Degree to provide a better life for me and my siblings. However, during the time my mother attended college in the summer, my sisters and I had the luxury of staying in Lansing with our aunt Lela. Aunt Lela was an awesome woman who loved family and planted tremendous seeds in my sisters and I. Was life always perfect growing up? NO! However, in spite of all the setbacks and obstacles that occurred in my pre-adult stages of life my mother did not quit and neither am I.

In addition to my mother as a role model, I had some really great grandparents. My grandmother was a praying woman of God. My grandparents were members of a Baptist church on the street we grew up on. They made us go to Sunday school, Vacation Bible School and church on Sundays. My grandmother had her favorite scripture, Psalms 23, posted on the refrigerator. She always said that the Lord was our Shepherd, and we would not want for anything, as long as we followed the words of the Lord.

My grandmother owned her own beauty salon. My grandfather built a salon attached to their home for my grandmother's convenience. I really believe that it was for my grandfather's convenience. My grandmother always made sure when my grandfather came home from work he had a hot home cooked meal waiting for him.

My grandmother loved designing clothes, hats, and of course shopping. She always took us shopping in Detroit and we loved going. She was a well put together, couture woman. She was so beautiful inside and out! I absolutely adored her.

Remember, we are talking about being the best You! "So Please Don't Judge Me and I won't Judge You!"

My grandfather was very money smart. He didn't believe in using credit cards. He always believed that if you did not have the money to purchase something that meant you did not need to purchase the item. My grandfather always paid cash for his new cars. He worked at a foundry and he was a Union Steward. As the Union Steward, he traveled to business meetings and would sometimes take me and my grandmother along. She loved to go shopping with the other ladies that traveled with their husbands.

As a teenager, I spent the majority of my free time in the company of my grandparents. I loved being with them. I loved fashion, baking and shopping with my grandmother. I also loved listening to my grandfather share his different stories about being in the army and traveling. I knew that my purpose had to be with people, fashion and/or modeling. I loved reading the fashion magazines, creating collages and I really enjoyed watching the black & white movies with all the high fashion.

When I was a young adult around 20 years old, I realized that I didn't really like myself. During this time I was going to college just taking classes that did not really define my future purpose or passion. I was taking basic and biblical classes at Kalamazoo Valley Community College. There wasn't anything wrong with taking classes, but there was something wrong with not knowing the path that I really wanted to take in life.

I joined a modeling group and learned some basic modeling. I really enjoyed that short time in my life. That actually helped me build confidence in simply being me!

While I was in college, I lived with my boyfriend and he played basketball. We had lots of parties, and invited all types of friends over to our home.

Unfortunately, when you don't know who you are, you compromise and try and do just about anything. With that being said, I began drinking and experimenting with drugs. It did not take me very long to figure out that, there was nothing in that atmosphere to define any type of positive purpose or direction in life.

I enjoyed finding vintage & second hand stores. I worked in a few retail stores in my young twenties and I really enjoyed selling shoes, clothes and handbags. I was an excellent salesperson; I had become a personal shopper for several of my customers who came in the store asking for me specifically. I got my excitement and motivation from assisting my customers. I loved listening to what their requests were and solving their problems. I created dynamic outfits that allowed them to look and feel unbelievably beautiful. My passion for assisting clients defined me as a personal shopper.

I dropped out of college, and started focusing on working to pay the rent and supplement my shopping habit. My next career assignment was property leasing for residential apartment complexes. I loved assisting people find their homes. That was very rewarding for me; it was very similar to helping someone define their fashion style. I had a natural gift for decorating homes and people. I do believe you are what you decorate.

Remember, we are talking about being the best You! "So Please Don't Judge Me and I won't Judge You!"

At the age of 22, I was pregnant and got married two months before the baby was due! Sometimes we try to do the right thing for everyone else, but it may not be the right decision for our life at that time. I was married for about 6 ½ years and it finally ended in a divorce two babies later with a bumped & bruised self-esteem. However, during the 6 ½ years of marriage we were separated for at least 2 years.

My self-esteem was bruised because at times I allowed negative thoughts of having children, with no college education or a good job make me think less of myself. And let's not forget, moving around from place to place each year when my lease was up, because I always needed to save money on the rent.

Right before I determined it was time to move on with my life, I found myself pregnant again. I made the decision to have an abortion. I learned that you never make any decisions for your life when you are angry and afraid. That is a time when you are so vulnerable and unclear with your thoughts. I beat myself up for a very long time for having an abortion and not doing what was right for my life at that time. There were times when my self-esteem would get so low I would have thoughts of suicide, but I remembered the scripture "Greater is He that is in me, than he that is in the world." I learned at an early age how to speak positive confessions about myself, which quickly removes negative thoughts.

I had to file for a divorce on my own, because I couldn't afford a lawyer. I began doing some research and found out about a program where you represent yourself as an attorney. I decided to go ahead with that program and it took me two months to organize the paperwork to file with the court system. My divorce was finalized in 6 months. Out of 7 years of marriage we probably lived together for a total of five years. We were just, two young people who were uneducated about marriage and unprepared for such a covenant commitment.

The most beautiful part of the divorce was having two children. The unfortunate part of it was that my oldest daughter, who was 6 at the time, was very attached to her father. My ex-husband moved to New York and of course he was too far away to play an active role in either one of my children's lives. I was a single parent long before the divorce was official. I managed the majority of the parenting activities, acting out the role of a single mother.

After my divorce was final, I started taking college courses to help build my confidence. At that time I wasn't 100% sure what I wanted to be when I grew up, but I knew I wanted to be an entrepreneur. I enjoyed the idea of entrepreneurship because there were no limits to the salary you could make. I'd be able to determine my outcomes in the business by what I put into it. I could serve my customers with the best customer service without anyone telling me that is just too much or it's not necessary. I could determine when I needed a vacation and for how long. My true calling is entrepreneurship!

I was working at an apartment complex as a Leasing Consultant and I enjoyed my job. I became so good at leasing & marketing that I decided to create a business called Unlimited Lifestyles. It was a marketing business to train other Leasing Consultants on how to market & lease the apartments to prospective future tenants. The ultimate goal was to remain at a 100% occupied with a waiting list for future residents and create a positive community culture within the complex. I won several awards and contests by being "blind shopped" by the company I worked for and the competition. "Blind-Shopping" means that they sent out secret shoppers to apply for apartments and I was rated on customer service, knowledge, follow-up, etc.

Eventually, it was time for me to go back to school and complete the college degree I'd started years ago. I finally began to think about what I really wanted to do with my life. I took a class called Eliminating Self Defeating Behaviors. Through that class I was able to begin eliminating any negativity I felt towards myself. Some of the negative behaviors were fears from my past and blaming others for my poor choices. I learned that I had to face my fears head on and defeat them. I also had to own up to any negative choices I made and make a decision to not allow the decisions to contaminate my future.

Also during this time, I was asked to teach a parenting class part-time to teen mothers and that was one of the most rewarding assignments I have ever completed, for free. I loved sharing information that worked for me. I shared the benefits and mistakes I made from poor choices with the single mothers. It was most rewarding for me when they took the information I shared and applied it to their individual situation. Some of the women truly wanted a better life for their future.

Based on my past mistakes, I made a choice to learn how to love me for who I was. I really began to reflect on my life and what I needed to do to provide the best life for myself and my 2 daughters. I knew that I was created to make a difference. I was in search of my purpose and I began to search for my identity in self-help books and magazines. I went to hear several speakers who were very positive and motivating. I began going to church and limited how much time I utilized in focusing on things that didn't really matter. I knew that I wanted to be a business woman so; I decided to research colleges that would not only help me meet this goal, but would also be convenient for me to work full-time and take college classes as a single mother.

While on my way to pursuing purpose, I had some setbacks- As a result of poor choices in money management, I experienced the "bad credit monster" that attacked my finances. I started reading several books on credit repair and learning about the value of your credit score. I wrote down a goal for my credit score, at that time my goal was 700. The first thing I did was pull my credit report and learned how to read it. I made sure all the credit on the report listed did in fact belong to me. After that I started calling the negative accounts to negotiate lowering the interest rates and making affordable monthly payments.

Just a side note on credit: I was in about $750,000.00 of debt in 2008. However my faith in God brought me out and four years later I am still standing and walking with my head held high, because I am somebody! I am not defined by things! I define the things that I allow to come into my atmosphere! I know when to trust God! I know when to be still, I know when to move!

Remember, we are talking about being the best You! "So Please Don't Judge Me and I won't Judge You!"

I wanted to give you just a little background on me before we begin to define U. One of the most important steps I took was making a choice to live my life as a Kingdom Builder! Once I made that decision many years ago I finally got to understand who I was and got a glimpse of what I was created to be. I believe we were all born to make a difference in someone's life!

Let's explore what worked for me and what I believe will work for you. Please give it a try and send me an email at beingu4real@gmail.com.

BE U
&
DO U
4REAL!

Chapter 1

Define "U"

You must first DEFINE U to BE U and then DO U. A good friend of mine always says "stay in your own lane" and that is exactly what this journey encompasses. But the first step is finding the right lane or learning to DEFINE U.

Take a moment and define U:

1. What past events in your life do you need to let go of and move on from to be U?

2. What were some of your favorite things you enjoyed doing as a child?

I was created to make a difference in the world!

3. Am I making a difference?

4. Is it a positive difference or a negative difference?

Take just a moment and write down what you're allowing to define you: *(Things can be labels, i.e. Gucci, Louis Vuitton, Prada, Chanel, Goodwill, Target, Sears, J.C. Penney, etc.)*

_____

_____

_____

5. What people are you allowing to define U?

6. Why do you allow people or things to define U?

7. How do you feel about other people's definition of U?

8. What groups are U trying to fit in with?

**Your authentic uniqueness
empowers your true identity!**

JOURNALING THE BEST U!

Chapter 2

Defining Me With No Limits

This is going to be fun and thought provoking: Close your eyes and meditate about what you want to be, realistically, without counting up the cost to make it happen...

You can write it below or write it in a notebook.

_____

_____

_____

_____

_____

_____

_____

_____

Now, let's create a list of the items you wrote about that you would actually like to see in your life.

Count up the cost, for example if you wrote a College Professor and you don't have any college education, first you need to research colleges and begin to decide what you would like to teach. How much is tuition? What grants and scholarships are available? Write up your confession and begin taking classes.

_____

_____

_____

_____

_____

_____

_____

_____

_____

_____

Next create a list showing the cost and steps you wrote. For example, one of your goals is you would like to become an entrepreneur, you need to first decide what type of business you want to own. Do you have the knowledge for the business? Go and speak with other successful people who are business owners, and ask them questions about how they started their business. I always try to find out something about the person that I'm interviewing before they give up some of their valuable time to sow into my future and give them a nice gift. It could be a gift card to a coffee shop, restaurant or even just a nice thank you note. Remember it is always important to respect other peoples time.

_____

_____

_____

_____

_____

_____

_____

_____

_____

_____

Frame Your Future with this page as your picture frame to what you listed above!

Defining your authentic identity: Loving the U God created. Living, being and doing the original U, no matter the cost.

JOURNALING THE BEST U!

_____

_____

_____

_____

_____

_____

_____

_____

_____

_____

_____

_____

_____

_____

Chapter 3

My Self-Esteem

Self-esteem: How I feel about myself?

1. Do I like what I see when I look in the mirror?

2. If the answer to the question is "No" - Am I willing to make some changes?

3. Does my image play a role in how I feel about myself?

4. Am I confident being me?

5. What necessary adjustments do I need to make?

6. Do I need assistance making the adjustments? If yes what type of assistance do I need?

7. How soon should I begin making the adjustments and or improvements for my life?

Examples: Do I need to lose some weight? Change my hair or makeup? Do I need to find a signature perfume scent? Do I like my clothes? Do I watch too much TV? Do I need to study and read more?

Write down what you need, and if you need help accomplishing the changes you would like to become.

_____

_____

_____

_____

_____

_____

_____

_____

In order to live an authentic, confident life it is imperative that you make a decision to no longer look at your past failures as hurdles, but tests that come to strengthen your future.

BE U
&
DO U
4REAL!

JOURNALING THE BEST U!

_____

_____

_____

_____

_____

_____

_____

_____

_____

_____

_____

_____

_____

_____

Chapter 4

Courageous U

It takes courage to define who you are for real. Are you ready to begin the process? You can't worry about other people's opinions about who you are. Remember you are an authentic individual and you have been uniquely created by God. There is no one else like you. You are the original masterpiece. You are a brilliant diamond with many intricate facets.

To live an authentic life you must choose to focus on your current position instead of your past failures. You must choose to take the mask off!

A confident woman knows who she is in Christ. She has a spiritual relationship that nurtures all their other relationships. "I praise you because I am fearfully and wonderfully made; your works are wonderful and I know that full well." -Psalm 139: 14

Webster's Dictionary defines courage as bold, brave & confident.

Always begin by praying and asking God who you are, and studying your Bible.

1. What motivates you?

2. What are you passionate about?

3. What are your gifts & talents?

4. When you look in the mirror do you see a woman or a girl?

5. Write a confession about yourself and say it every day.

A Sample Confession:
I am a confident, highly favored and powerful woman of God. My image & self-esteem are intact and I love who I am. I look into the mirror boldly every morning and I command my atmosphere with the words from my mouth. I have an optimistic & positive attitude and I take authority fulfilling my authentic purpose and destiny. No good thing shall be withheld from me! I am a lender & not a borrower! I am a Kingdom Builder for life!

Remember it is very important that you define you! It is a process that you will need to work towards every day. Don't be concerned about other people's ideas and opinions of who you are as you begin to meditate about your life. This part of the process is very important!

Just be 4Real with you! Remember you are unique and you have been fearfully and wonderfully made. You are somebody very special!

Choose an accountability partner or coach you can trust or send me emails and I will be happy to coach you!

Silence the negativity that comes to suffocate your purpose & destiny!

BE U
&
DO U
4REAL!

JOURNALING THE BEST U!

Chapter 5

Be U

Imagine that you are the CEO of your life and you need to make some executive changes to accomplish your goals and dreams. If you don't make the necessary changes to your company, you may run the risk of your company going into bankruptcy.

Being the best you God created, starts off with a written vision of how you want to see your life. Write a vision for every area of your life. You need a vision for your home, image, purpose, education, profession, job, children, husband, marriage, self-esteem, etc.

It is very important that you surround yourself with people who celebrate you. Your dream is something that you need to be very careful with whom you share it with. Everyone that appears to be with you is not always assigned to be with you. Be aware of destiny thieves & dream sabotagers because they come to stop you from being the best you.

In Luke 1:39, Mary visited Elizabeth; Mary was the mother of Jesus and Elizabeth was the mother of John the Baptist. Elizabeth greeted Mary and said to her "Blessed are you among women, and blessed is the child you will bare!" Mary spent about three months with Elizabeth and then she returned home. I believe that Mary stayed with Elizabeth because she was assigned to her purpose and destiny. Elizabeth coached and prepared Mary for the greatest purpose of all to fulfill, by birthing Jesus into the world. The number three signifies Divine Perfection!

The sooner you begin taking the steps towards becoming the CEO for your life, the sooner you begin to walk in your defined purpose and destiny. Remember that everyone operates by the same timing system. The longer you put off being who you really are, the longer it takes for you to manifest your dreams for your life. Remember a delay is not denial!

Habakkuk 2:2,3 states it plainly ,"…and the Lord answered me and said, Write the vision, and make it plain upon tables, that he may run that reads it. For the vision is yet for an appointed time, but at the end it shall speak, and not lie: though it tarry, wait for it; because it will surely come, it will not tarry."

It's time to take the necessary steps to BE U:

1. **Identify** your dreams, visions, or goals.

2. **Define** smaller goals or steps that are part of the bigger picture.

3. **Take Action!**

4. **Evaluate** where you are and then readjust.

5. **Celebrate the Authentic YOU!**

God has a great investment in YOU, don't miss out on your return!

BE U
&
DO U
4REAL!

JOURNALING THE BEST U!

Chapter 6

Do U

Now the best part begins by taking the necessary action steps towards being who you were created to be. You can do this because you have written your visions, confessions and goals to be and do the best you.

I want to remind you of just a few people in the Bible who had to take action steps that made a huge difference in their lives and in the life of many others.

Let's begin with a short paraphrased story about some of our great leaders from the Bible:

Sarah: She went many years before she gave birth to her baby. She was very old and if you looked at the circumstances, including her age, who would have ever believed that God would have told her she was going to give birth to a baby at such an old age, but she gave birth to a son.

Esther: She risked her life to save her people by pretending to be a different culture in order to be considered for the possibility of marrying the King. She went against all odds to use her voice & position to save the lives of her people. However, most of all she had to put her faith and trust in

God. Esther's trust in God saved the people!

Mary: She had to believe God that she was going to give birth to a savior without ever having any type of relationship with a man. She was a woman who did not have sex with her husband, but she told him she was pregnant with the baby Jesus! Can you imagine telling your husband something like that and you were a virgin and you have not even slept with him yet! You better know that you are hearing from God. In those days to become pregnant without a husband or to commit adultery could bring you to death.

The Woman with the Issue of Blood: She had been bleeding for many years; she heard that a savior was coming into the city and she had decided that if she could just touch the hem of his garment she would be healed. She had to take action and believe that this was going to be the miracle she had been waiting for and because she believed, she received her blessing immediately. She took action with her faith and was healed!

Job: This is one of my favorite stories in the Bible, Job lost his wife, children and everything he had. He went through so much persecution all the way until the end of the book. Job repented to God, forgave his friends and interceded for them. Job was immediately blessed with more than he had lost.

There are many, many more stories in the Bible and you probably know people who have their own stories of how they overcame by making a decision to be the best they could be, by not allowing any of their failures or walking in unforgiveness, stop them from fulfilling their purpose and destiny. We have to walk in Love & Forgiveness to Be & Do the Best Us!

"Don't let anything deter your dreams and overpower your passions. Go for what God has placed in your heart!"
- Bishop T. D. Jakes

BE U
&
DO U
4REAL!

JOURNALING THE BEST U!

Chapter 7

Be U & Do U 4Real

When you identify and eliminate at least 90% of the negatives in your life, the 10% left will give you a clearer picture of the positive directions in your path. Now you can walk in your true identity of the Proverbs 31 Woman.

*There are 31 Characteristics of a **Virtuous Woman**:*

1. Blameless
2. Valuable
3. Trustworthy
4. Good and True Nature
5. Highly Favored
6. Leader
7. Considerate
8. Versatile
9. Healthy
10. Joyful - efficient
11. Watchful - cautious
12. Courageous
13. Charitable
14. Generous
15. Fearless

16. Creative
17. Refined in taste
18. Respected - popular
19. Prosperous
20. Dependable - honest
21. Confident - hopeful
22. Wise - discreet
23. Kind - understanding
24. Integrity
25. Energetic - active
26. An ideal wife and mother
27. Honored by her family
28. Excels in virtue
29. God - fearing - humble
30. Deserving - successful
31. Honored by the public

After reviewing the list of characteristics, which of these do you exemplify?

_____

_____

_____

_____

_____

_____

Scriptures

Courage:
Wait on the Lord: be of good courage, and he shall strengthen thine heart: wait, I say, on the Lord.
Psalms 27:14

Faith:
For you walk by faith and not by sight. *2 Corinthians 5:7*

Forgiveness:
For if ye forgive men their trespasses, your heavenly Father will also forgive you. *Matthew 6:14*

Judge not, and ye shall not be judged: condemn not, and ye shall not be condemned: forgive, and ye shall be forgiven. *Luke 6:35-38*

Guidance:
The steps of a good man are ordered by the Lord: And he delighted in his way. *Psalm 37:23*

Help in Trouble:
Many are the afflictions of the righteous: But the Lord delivered him out of them all. *Psalms 34:19*

Holy Spirit:
Behold, I will pour out my Spirit unto you, I will make known my words unto you. *Proverbs 1:23*

And I will pray the father, and he shall give you another

Comforter, that he may abide with you forever; Even the Spirit of truth; whom the world cannot receive, because it sees him not, neither know him: but ye know him; for he dwelleth with you, and shall be in you. *John 14: 16, 17*

Honesty:
You shall not steal, neither deal falsely, neither lie one to another. *Leviticus 19:11*

A false balance is abomination to the Lord: but a just weight is his delight. *Proverbs 11:1*

Hope:
Be ye of good courage, and he shall strengthen your heart, all ye that hope in the Lord. *Psalm 31:24*

Jealousy:
Be not thou envious against evil men, neither desire to be with them. *Proverbs 24:1*

And he said unto his disciples; therefore I say unto you, take no thought for your life, what ye shall eat; neither for the body, what ye shall put on. The life is more than meat, and the body is more than raiment. *Luke 12:22, 23*

Long Life:
My son, forget not my law, but let thine heart keep my commandments: For length of days, and long life, and peace, shall they add to thee. *Proverbs 3:1, 2*

Brotherly Love:
He that loveth not knoweth not God; for God is love.
I John 4:7, 8

Beloved, if God so loved us, we ought also to love one another. *I John 4:11*

God's Love:
For God so loved the world, that he gave his only begotten Son, that whosoever believeth in him should not perish, but have everlasting life. *John 3:16*

Delight thyself also in the Lord; and he shall give thee the desires of thine heart. *Psalm 37:4*

Because he hath set his love upon me, therefore will I deliver him: I will set him on high, because he hath known my name. *Psalm 91:14*

Money:
But thou shalt remember the Lord thy God: for it is he that gives thee power to get wealth, that he may establish his covenant which he sware unto thy fathers, as it is this day. *Deuteronomy 8:18*

A faithful man shall abound with blessings: but he that maketh haste to be rich shall not be innocent. *Proverbs 28:20*

Better is little with the fear of the Lord than great treasure and trouble therewith. *Proverbs 15:16*

Beloved I wish above all things that you should prosper and be in good health. *III John 1:2*

BE U
&
DO U
4REAL!

JOURNALING THE BEST U!

Chapter 8

Unstoppable U

I have determined that as long as I have breath and life in my body, I will continue to define my authentic purpose & destiny that God created me to fulfill. I am celebrating a second marriage with a Godly husband of 20 years. We are a blended family with 5 adult children and 11 grandchildren. My husband and I have been entrepreneurs since the mid 90's. He's an expert in the stock market, credit and money management, planning for retirement, weatherization & construction. He is an excellent husband, father, grandfather, leader and gardener. We have a ministry, we started, to help marriages called **unstoppablefamilies.com**. We have trained and written curriculums in Remarriage, Marriage & Premarital Classes. We believe the family is under attack and we want to empower, educate and provide the tools to stop the attack on the family.

I have a Bachelor's Degree in Management & Organizational Development and Master's Degree in Family Studies. I am the President of a Women's Entrepreneurial Group with a current membership of 100 women and growing. I have a Ministers Training certificate and I've written a program to build a strong self-esteem in women. I can confidently say I am free from having low self-esteem and I want to help other women become permanently free. I'm licensed in Real Estate and I have owned my own company, written foreclosure prevention manuals, provided training & education in home buying, credit repair, homelessness prevention and other classes.

Our prayers are that our children fulfill their God given purpose & destiny. My two oldest granddaughters are honor roll students in their school. We have a family confession on our wall and we stand on the scripture, 3 John 1:2 as a family. We believe that all our family is saved and they are going to fulfill their God given purpose & destiny with our love and support.

This is the conclusion of the first part of my story at the age of 50, and I believe once I decided to Be Me & Do Me 4REAL, then I respectfully earned the rights to share my story to help someone else with writing their story!

BE U
&
DO U
4REAL!

JOURNALING THE BEST U!

My Dearest Readers,

I am very excited that you took the time out of your busy schedule to read this book. I thank you & celebrate you as you define the Best, Authentic You. You were created to make a difference with your uniqueness!

I love what Jeremiah 1:5 says about us, for I know the thoughts and plans I had for you, before you were born! That means that God knew what your purpose was before you were created!

Remember to always Be U & Do U 4Real!

Carmen Thomas
unstoppablefamilies.com

JOURNALING THE BEST U!

_____

_____

_____

_____

_____

_____

_____

_____

_____

_____

_____

_____

_____

_____

ABOUT CARMEN THOMAS

As a native of Albion, MI, Carmen Thomas, alumna of Spring Arbor College holds a Master's Degree in Family Studies and Bachelor's Degree in Management & Organizational Development. Carmen is the Director and Organizer of the Meetups Group, "Authentic Women Walking In Purpose," proficient in ministry training and a "self-esteem" expert. Mrs. Thomas is a highly sought after speaker who travels the world inspiring, motivating, encouraging and empowering at various seminars, conferences and community events. In addition, Carmen teaches numerous topics, including but not limited to: foreclosure prevention, credit repair, home buying, marriage & family and self-esteem & purpose.

With combined experience of over 20 years in Real Estate as a Marketing Specialist, Leasing Consultant, Office Manager, Sales Manager, Foreclosure Prevention and Home Education Coach, Owner of a Real Estate Company, Commercial & Residential Property Management and Sales, Carmen has proven to be an expert in the field and asset to the profession. She has diligently served her community as the President of The Women's Council of Realtors - Lansing Chapter, Michigan Association of Realtors, Circle of Excellence, South Lansing Community Development Association, in her local church and as the Ambassador for "Project: It's Still Possible." She has also received numerous certifications and recognition by her peers.

Carmen is very active in supporting and sponsoring community events and has a heart for women, families and the homeless. Carmen's mission is to educate, motivate and empower every individual she meets to do the impossible.

For more information on Carmen or booking information email: beingu4real@gmail.com or visit www.unstoppablefamilies.com.